Bread and Milk

by Melissa Gressok
illustrated by Jannie Ho

Practice Decodable 33

McGraw Hill Education

Bothell, WA • Chicago, IL • Columbus, OH • New York, NY

MHEonline.com

Send all inquiries to:
McGraw-Hill Education
8787 Orion Place
Columbus, OH 43240

ISBN: 978-0-02-145349-8
MHID: 0-02-145349-7

Printed in China

8 9 10 11 12 DSS 27 26 25 24 23

Jeff read, "Bread, jam, milk."
Then he headed back.

Jeff spread jam on bread.

Ann said, "Milk is not in the fridge!"

"I spilled it as I headed back," said Jeff.

"I was hot," Jeff added.
His hand was at his head.

Then Ann spotted the milk.
Ann grinned.